by Robert Wes

ISBN 978-0-9552061-7-7

Inspiring Places Publishing
2 Down Lodge Close
Alderholt
Fordingbridge
SP6 3JA
e-mail
robert.westwood3@btinternet.com
Acknowledgements:
Photo on page 19 by kind permission of
Nothe Fort Museum
Art work page 39 by Jennifer Westwood

Other titles by Inspiring Places:
Fossils and Rocks of the Jurassic Coast
Ancient Dorset
Dark Age Dorset
Day Tours in the East of Dorset
Mysterious Places of Dorset
Mystery Big Cats of Dorset
Smugglers' Dorset
Buy on-line at: **www.inspiringplaces.co.uk**

Printed by Hobbs the Printers, Totton

Contents

Front cover: Hambledon Hill
Rear Cover: The Abbot's Porch, Cerne Abbas

Introduction

Reminders of its rich history are everywhere in Dorset. Castles, abbeys, manor houses and ancient monuments draw tourists from all over the world. Although it has always been a largely rural, agricultural county, its proximity to such major centres as Salisbury and Winchester, and its important seaports has meant that it has featured in many defining periods of Britain's history.

At the beginning of the second millennium, following turbulent times when the Vikings were an ever present menace, peace had been restored by the strong Saxon kings of Wessex. Dorset was enjoying a relatively peaceful and prosperous period when Duke William of Normandy invaded.

This book deals with events after the Norman Conquest. It does not seek to give a complete history of the county, rather to pick out significant and important episodes and to direct the interested visitor to places where this colourful history is celebrated.

Above: From the ramparts of the famous Iron Age hillfort of Maiden Castle a sheep gazes over Dorset's ancient county town, Dorchester.

Left: Cerne Abbas seen from the top of the Giant.

The Normans in Dorset

Dorset, before the Conquest, was a thriving agricultural shire. Divided into 39 "Hundreds" for administrative purposes, it was a land of small villages, meadows and mills, with several well defended "burghs" such as Shaftesbury and Wareham. It had seen its fair share of trouble in the preceding two centuries, often under threat from Viking raiders, but a succession of strong kings had turned Wessex into a powerful and settled state. Further Viking incursions threw it once more into turmoil until peace was restored, perversely, by the Danish king, Canute.

News of the Norman invasion must have spread fear through the manors and villages of Dorset. Some no doubt hoped that they would be able to carry on their rural existence much as before, but prolonged outbreaks of resistance put paid to those hopes. A serious rebellion in the West Country meant a Norman army marched through Dorset, doing much damage on the way. Saxon thanes were dispossessed and Normans loyal to the king rewarded with their vacant manors. In 1085 the list of Dorset landowners in the Domesday Book shows vast estates were owned by the king, the church [including a number of French abbeys] and Norman lords. A few Saxon thanes were left holding small pockets of land; perhaps these were people who had collaborated with the invaders in some way or just kept their heads down!

Resentment of the Norman oppressors was understandably strong and it was never going to be easy for them to impose their rule,

The Norman church at Studland

Above: Castle Hill, Cranborne, site of the Norman motte and bailey

vastly outnumbered as they were. King William's brutality in putting down rebellions is well documented, but this was only part of his strategy. Leaving relatively few Normans in charge of manors created some dangerous situations. Consequently they embarked on a spree of castle building, often strong timber constructions on top of an artificial mound or "motte". There were a number of these in Dorset and their sites can still be seen. A good example is Castle Hill in Cranborne, a beautiful spot, now wooded and overlooking the village which had an important abbey. There is a tragic story attached to the abbey and the Norman Conquest; a Saxon nobleman called Brihtric, who was responsible for enlarging the abbey, once spurned the advances of William's future wife, Matilda, while on a diplomatic mission to Normandy. She did not forgive him and had William seize the abbey and throw Brihtric into prison where he died. Conveniently William was also able to seize about 15 000 acres belonging to Brihtric. No doubt this picture was repeated all across the county as other excuses were found to seize the estates of the Saxon thanes.

Many other motte and bailey castles were built but the Normans' chief strongholds were situated in the old Saxon burghs. Thus important castles were built at Christchurch, Wareham and Dorchester. The value of the site at Corfe was recognised and in the north of the county a substantial castle was later built at Sherborne. The main purpose of these castles was to protect the small number of Norman settlers from their Saxon neighbours and to deter them from harbouring thoughts of rebellion. Christchurch, Corfe and Sherborne Castles still remain and are all worth a visit.

Christchurch Castle

Initially a motte was constructed near the mill stream and the Saxon mill. This would have been topped by a timber stronghold. As well as protecting the local Normans, this castle guarded the entrance to two navigable rivers, the Stour and Avon. It would have offered some protection for the important settlement at Old Sarum. The present stone keep was built around 1300, perhaps for this very reason. Henry I gave the castle to the de Redvers family in 1100 and it was they who built the famous Constable's Hall, which now provides the backdrop for a quintessentially English scene, the site of the Christchurch bowling green.

Although it did not witness any great siege during medieval times it did its job well. During the Hundred Years War, when many neighbouring coastal towns were ravaged by French raiders, Christchurch remained intact. After the inevitable siege in the Civil War, Parliament ordered the castle slighted and the walls pulled down.

Below: Constable's Hall, Christchurch Castle

Above: Corfe Castle seen from the chalk ridge to the east

Corfe Castle

Corfe Castle is justly world famous. Some castles, like Tintagel, boast a fairy-tale location, others, like Christchurch, have obvious strategic value; some, like Corfe, have both. A lucky combination of erosional factors has led to a gap in the ridge of chalk that divides the Isle of Purbeck from Poole Harbour. In this gap is a ready made motte on which to build a fortress. Anyone who has seen the castle in early morning or evening light "floating" in a sea of mist will testify that it is one of the most magical sights England's heritage can offer.

William I began strengthening the original Saxon stronghold but it was under King John that Corfe grew in importance. It was one of the king's favourite residences and the centre of a royal hunting forest. He also used it to house some of his political prisoners and for his treasury. By then Corfe was a little "out of the way", no longer an important defence against raiders from the Purbeck coast, it was an ideal site to store things safely! Like Christchurch, Corfe too was slighted after a Civil War siege; more of that later.

Sherborne Castle

Sherborne Castle was built in the 12th century for Roger of Caen, Bishop of Salisbury. From humble beginnings, Roger rose to great power and wealth after winning the confidence of Henry I. Although not much remains of the castle, again due to post Civil War slighting, it is nevertheless a picturesque ruin, set in lovely parkland.

Right and below:
Old Sherborne Castle showing the main entrance across a formidable moat, and the ruined remains inside with the castle well which was sunk deep into the rock on which it was built.

Civil War in Dorset

The "Anarchy" of Stephen and Matilda

Dorset has seen its fair share of violent conflict. Even before the Roman invasion Iron Age tribes lived in heavily defended hillforts. When the Romans left Saxon armies replaced the legions and when they were defeated a Norman army ravaged the peaceful countryside. Dorset's history seems to present a rhythmical pattern of peaceful and relatively prosperous interludes followed by violent upheaval. As well as invading armies Dorset has been the stage for civil war on a number of occasions. Perhaps the conflicts between Charles I and Parliament and the Monmouth Rebellion are best known but Dorset witnessed bitter fighting in another dispute for the control of England in the 12th century.

History books recall that Stephen succeeded his uncle Henry I as king of England. Henry's only legitimate son, William, had been drowned in the famous incident of the "White Ship" in 1120, but Henry had made his barons, including Stephen, Count of Mortain, swear to uphold his daughter Matilda as heir. On the king's death in 1135 Stephen seized the throne. This was not as roundly condemned as might be thought, Matilda had married Geoffrey of Anjou without any

Below: Wareham, the white house is on the site of the Norman castle.

Above: Christchurch Harbour from Hengistbury Head

consultation in England. Also, Geoffrey had tried to assert his claims in Normandy and been thrown out. Thus Matilda was in no position to challenge Stephen.

All went fairly well for the king for the first four years, but then some trouble with several bishops coincided with the arrival in England of Matilda and her half-brother Robert, earl of Gloucester. Unrest spread and England quickly became divided by the two camps. Matilda had a powerful ally in Ranulf, earl of Chester and unrest turned into civil war. Throughout the conflict Dorset saw a considerable amount of intrigue and fighting.

Henry I had given Christchurch Castle to Richard de Redvers. It was an important strategic location, controlling the entrance to two navigable rivers, the Stour and Avon. On his death it passed to his son, Baldwin de Redvers, the first earl of Devon. He had refused to accept Stephen from the start and had quickly seized Exeter castle. A prolonged siege by Stephen took Exeter back and Baldwin was expelled from England. Baldwin returned in 1138 and immediately seized Wareham and Corfe Castle where he was besieged by Stephen. Any visitor to Corfe Castle will not be surprised that the siege was unsuccessful.

Robert of Gloucester took over Wareham after he returned from a visit to Normandy in 1142. Stephen mounted another siege, again unsuccessful.

Sherborne Castle too features in this civil war. Under Henry I, Roger de Caen, Bishop of Salisbury had become the second most powerful man in England. He built a number of fine castles, including one at Sherborne. Stephen suspected him of plotting with Matilda, had him arrested and his castles confiscated. According to legend this led to the bishop issuing a curse on any secular owners of the castle. Amongst others, the curse is said to have worked its spell on Sir Walter Raleigh! Whatever the truth of this Edward III returned the castle to the Bishopric of Salisbury in 1337.

As with any civil war, some violent episodes related not to grand strategic plans by the major protagonists, but to individuals sensing an opportunity to benefit themselves. Such a man was Walter de Pinckney who harboured a grudge against Robert of Gloucester and took his chance to seize Christchurch Castle. This was not a popular move with the people of Christchurch and he was subsequently hacked to death by an angry mob in the priory precincts in 1145.

Eventually Dorset and England settled down and the charismatic Stephen was confirmed as king, but not before Matilda had secured the succession for her son Henry.

Above: The Constable's Hall, Christchurch Castle, seen from across the mill stream.

Left: The Norman keep of Christchurch Castle

The Black Death

In the century between 1180 and 1280 Dorset and much of the south of England experienced a relative golden age. The climate had begun to enter a warm cycle at the beginning of the 12th century and the long, warm summers combined with sufficient rainfall ensured that there was food for all. Life expectancy began to rise and the population level rose to nearly 6 million, a figure not reached again until the 18th century. Most of this population was in central southern England. Dorset was once again a thriving agricultural region with rich abbeys and prosperous manors.

In the early 14th century things were to change dramatically. Firstly, the climate began to change again, this time entering into a cooler cycle. Coincidentally, the climate was also affected by huge volcanic eruptions in Indonesia that resulted in terrible summers in 1316 and 1317. The lack of sun meant that crops did not ripen and there was widespread famine. Then, in 1348, a humble merchant ship docking in the port of Melcombe Regis [now Weymouth] was to initiate a chain of events that would devastate the population of Dorset and England.

It is generally accepted that the Black Death came to England via the port of Weymouth when, on the 25th June 1348, a small merchant ship docked. The ship's rats were infected and it is thought fleas from the rats carried the bacteria which

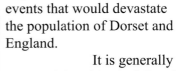

Left: The old harbour at Weymouth. It was here in 1348 that the plague arrived in England.
Opposite right: Ruined Knowlton church set in a Neolithic henge. It once served a thriving village.

were passed to humans when they were bitten. It may also be that the germs were carried in the air via rats' droppings. Within four days, the first deaths from the disease occurred in Weymouth.

It soon spread to the villages and hamlets around Weymouth causing many to head inland which, of course, further spread the disease. The village of West Chickerell has the dubious honour of being the first Dorset village to lose its priest; many more were to follow as the clergy tried in vain to nurse the sick. The coastal regions of Dorset appear to have been the worst hit, Portland particularly so. Here quarries were left abandoned and in 1352 Edward III issued orders restricting the movement of the people of Portland. Many villages were abandoned all over Dorset and the traces of some of these can still be seen today.

In June 2007, new evidence from Dorset was published which casts some doubt about whether the Black Death was in fact the Bubonic Plague as has traditionally been assumed. Court records from Gillingham in the north of the county show that most of the deaths there occurred in the winter of 1348/9, a time when the fleas should have been dormant. This has led to speculation that the disease may have been viral, perhaps similar to Ebola. It may be that, in a population already weakened by the effects of famine, other diseases took hold and added to the devastation caused by the plague.

Whatever the cause, viral or bacterial, and however it was transmitted, its rapid spread devastated the population. It is estimated that 30-40% of the population died and Dorset was one of the worst affected areas.

The Civil War 1642 - 1651

The English Civil War lasted from 1642 to 1651 when Charles II was defeated at the Battle of Worcester. It was a time of great hardship and much violence. Perhaps getting on for 100 000 men lost their lives in battle and thousands more perished through disease and famine. With a national population then of around 5 million it is clear the war had a devastating effect. The fact that Dorset suffered heavily is supported by the Clubmen's Rebellion when ordinary men, worn out and impoverished through endless conflict, banded together to oppose both sides and protect their county from further deprivation.

At the start of the war Dorset was largely controlled by Parliament. In particular the important ports were under Parliamentary control. It has been suggested that this was largely due to the rich merchants who anticipated better trade and more profits under a Parliamentary government. In the years following 1642 Dorset was to see a number of major engagements as well as several smaller sieges and skirmishes.

Sherborne Castle

Sherborne Castle figures prominently in the history of the Civil War. At the start of hostilities it was owned by Lord Digby, an advisor to the king. It soon became a base for the Marquis of Hertford who had been given

Above: The Cobb, Lyme Regis
Below left: "New" Sherborne Castle, home of Lord Digby. It was the
old castle behind it that was used as a defensive position.

the task of raising troops in the West Country. It was then besieged by Parliamentary troops under the Earl of Bedford. After some indecisive skirmishing Bedford withdrew to await reinforcements and the Marquis seized his chance to escape. However in April 1643 Royalist forces regained control of Sherborne.

The Royalists remained in charge at Sherborne until 1645 when a Parliamentary force under General Fairfax again besieged the castle. The defenders were commanded by Sir Lewis Dives, the brother-in-law of Lord Digby. The siege lasted 15 days, a testament to the strength of the castle, even in the days of gunpowder. Fairfax then ordered it to be pulled down so that it could not be used again. Sir Lewis was sent to the Tower of London.

Lyme Regis

By 1644 most of Dorset was in Royalist hands. Lyme Regis was an important Parliamentary stronghold. Although a relatively small port, it was nevertheless important strategically as a supply centre. In April 1644 Prince Maurice marched on Lyme with a force of about 6000 Royalists. He deployed them in an arc around the town and called on the

Above: Hambledon Hill, scene of the Dorset Clubmen's last stand.

defenders to surrender. They refused and a bitter siege ensued. Despite artillery bombardment, fire arrows and a number of attempts to storm the town, the siege dragged on. In June the Earl of Essex took it upon himself to bring reinforcements and Prince Maurice withdrew his men. The siege had lasted nearly two months and had cost hundreds of lives.

The Siege of Weymouth

Most major battles of the Civil War were either sieges or fought in open territory. Weymouth is unusual for being the scene of bitter street fighting. In February 1645 Weymouth was a relatively secure base for Parliament. Although the Royalists had been having some success in Dorset, Weymouth was protected by two impressive forts and had the respected Colonel William Sydenham in charge. However, a group of Royalists in the town came up with a plot that was very nearly successful and would result in the deaths of many on both sides.

The plot was basically that Royalists from Portland would simultaneously attack the forts while others would let a Royalist army from Sherborne into the town. The two forts fell but the army from Sherborne never materialised. In the attack Francis Sydenham, brother of the Governor, was fatally wounded. In the following days things got worse for the Parliamentarians. Not only did Sir Lewis Dive with his army from Sherborne arrive but so did Lord Goring with another 4500 troops. The garrison at Weymouth was now outnumbered over 4 to 1. Over two weeks of fighting were to follow with some bitter struggles in the streets of Weymouth. In the end the Parliamentary forces held on to the town, thanks in no small part to the gallantry and cunning of the Governor's younger brother Thomas Sydenham.

The Dorset Clubmen

By 1645 England had endured three years of bloody civil war. There had been several major battles and many minor ones. The many thousands of men in military service had to be paid and fed and, unsurprisingly, this caused great hardship for the rest of the population, particularly in rural communities where food stocks and crops were looted, requisitioned and ruined. A number of counties, Dorset among them, saw uprisings by groups of men opposed to both sides and utterly fed up with the war. Their intention was simply to protect their own villages and farmland. Many groups were led by clergymen and they armed themselves with whatever they could get hold of, knives, pitchforks and of course clubs. The fact that Dorset was one of the counties where bands of Clubmen formed tells us that the county had suffered much. It is perhaps unfortunate the Dorset Clubmen are famously remembered for an incident that appears somewhat comic.

In May 1645 around 4000 Clubmen gathered at Wimborne St. Giles and organised groups to seize army plunderers. This seems a sensible and effective measure to take to try and relieve some of the unnecessary suffering. Meeting trained troops head on in battle would have been suicide but harassing the armies in this way could have secured some bargaining power. In August 1645 some 2-4000 of the Dorset Clubmen had gathered on Hambledon Hill. Perhaps they intended to set up a camp of some sort from where they could go out and continue their operations. Unfortunately the Parliamentary army had just successfully concluded the siege of Sherborne Castle and a detachment of around 1000 soldiers under Oliver Cromwell was sent to deal with this perceived threat. The engagement was short lived, a few clubmen were killed and most fled. Cromwell rounded up about 500 and locked them in a nearby church for the night. In the morning he gave them a stern lecture and let them go. It is often quoted that he called them "poor, silly creatures", but it is surely an unfair description for these men who had

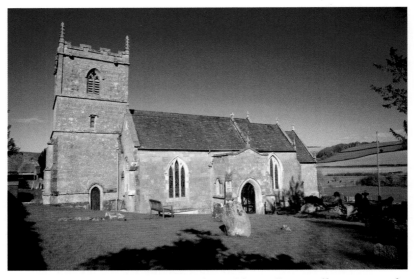

Above: The church at Shroton where Oliver Cromwell imprisoned some of the Dorset Clubmen overnight.

left to defend their homes against professional soldiers better trained and equipped than they were.

The Siege of Corfe Castle

Perhaps the most well-known episode of the Civil War in Dorset is the siege of Corfe Castle and the story of how heroic Lady Bankes led the defence of the castle against a vastly superior force.

Sir John Bankes, the Attorney General, had bought the castle in 1634. When hostilities broke out he remained loyal to the king. Dorset was deep in Parliamentary territory and it must have been obvious to their commanders that such a mighty fortress could prove a serious hindrance if it was allowed to stay in Royalist hands. Consequently, in 1643, the Parliamentarians under Sir Walter Erle besieged the castle. Sir John was away in Oxford and so it was left to Lady Bankes to organise the defence. She did this so well that the castle held out for six weeks, until they were relieved by a force commanded by the Earl of Caernarvon. Erle left in disarray, leaving much useful equipment behind.

By December 1645 most of the West Country was in Parliamentary hands, but Corfe remained as a thorn in the side. The time had come for a renewed effort to take the castle. Sir John Bankes had died suddenly in 1644 and so once again it was left to his wife to lead the defence. She declined a chance to escape and set about her task. Again the castle held out for weeks until in February 1646 an act of betrayal led to its downfall. An officer named Colonel Pitman set up negotiations about an exchange of prisoners, but in reality he was arranging to let attackers into the castle. Lady Bankes had no option but to surrender and she was allowed to leave with her honour intact. Parliament ordered the destruction of the castle and the ruins we see today are the result of this. It was more thoroughly destroyed than many castles; much of the stone was later used to rebuild the shattered village.

After the Restoration the estate was returned to the Bankes family who, unable to use the castle, built a splendid new home at Kingston Lacy. Today the National Trust own both properties and both are well worth a visit.

Many other smaller clashes took place in Dorset during the Civil War as the forces of Parliament attempted to capture isolated Royalist strongholds. One such engagement took place at Abbotsbury, the home of the Royalist Strangways family. In 1643 Parliamentary troops looted the manor and in 1644 a much larger force arrived to take the Royalist garrison commanded by Sir James Strangways. Some bitter fighting ensued and the church pulpit of St. Nicholas' still shows bullet holes from the encounter. The village was taken and another Royalist pocket of resistance was removed.

The Nothe Fort guarding the entrance to Weymouth Harbour; one of the forts attacked by Royalists - now a museum.

The Flight of Charles II from the Battle of Worcester

Charles I had been executed in 1649, the Monarchy abolished and England declared a Commonwealth. He had had the foresight to send his two eldest sons to France and so technically Charles II succeeded his father while in exile. In 1650 unrest amongst Scottish Presbyterians led them to invite Charles II to Scotland, to regain his throne with their help. Against the wishes of his most trusted servants he went. A wholly unsuccessful campaign ended in comprehensive defeat by Cromwell at the Battle of Worcester in 1651. Paradoxically, the events in the following weeks would forever enhance the reputation of the charismatic monarch.

Charles II's flight from the Battle of Worcester has passed into folklore as a classic tale of royalty disguised among ordinary people. Add to this the almost constant danger and the presence of mind, courage

and fortitude shown by a very young man, and it is no surprise that the story has been recounted many times in print.

After initially heading north from Worcester, Charles tried to leave the country from Bristol. When this failed he headed south to Dorset and this is where we pick up the story. He spent many subsequent days in Dorset before finally escaping back to France and his time here has led to many interesting and often amusing episodes.

The little village of Trent in north Dorset lies close to the border with Somerset. The manor here was owned by a staunch Royalist, Colonel Francis Wyndham, a hero who, since the war, had settled down to a life of rural obscurity. Although Parliamentary

Above: Part of the "Monarch's Way" at Pilsdon Pen. This long distance footpath follows the route taken by the king on his daring escape.

Above: The Cobb at Lyme Regis from where Charles hoped to sail. Left: The Queen's Arms in Charmouth, no longer an inn, also records an earlier famous visitor, Catharine of Aragon, in 1501.

troops were still scouring the countryside for the king Wyndham had no hesitation in not only hiding Charles and his companions but also took an active part in trying to secure a passage for the king from Lyme Regis. The predicament was made more dangerous because this part of Dorset was strongly pro Parliament and whilst he was hiding at Trent Charles had the unnerving experience of watching the villagers celebrate on hearing erroneous news that he had been killed at Worcester!

Within a few days Wyndham and Charles' companions had formulated what seemed a perfect plan. They had found a captain at Lyme Regis willing to take them to France on the pretext of wanting to claim some debts owed to them. They would go down to Charmouth the previous day and stay at an inn, leaving in the middle of the night. Here their imagination had also served them well; they had told the hostess that two lovers were eloping – Charles was to be the manservant. She loved the story and promised to tell no one. The plan was not only clever but daring. A reward for the capture of the king had recently been publicised and there was to be a fair at Lyme Regis the day they sailed, it would be packed with people.

They arrived at the Queen's Arms in Charmouth just after nightfall and prepared to wait until the small hours when a messenger would tell them the boat was ready at nearby Lyme. The hours passed and no word came. Worried, they hastily reviewed their plan. Charles and two others, including Colonel Wyndham, would make for Bridport, put up at an inn and wait for word as to what had gone wrong. This was more dangerous than expected; the town was full of soldiers but on Charles' insistence they rode calmly past the troops to the best inn. Here, as the servant, Charles led the horses to the stable, already crowded with soldiers. Just as he thought he had come through this test of nerves the hostler announced that he recognised his face. It says a lot for the king's nerve and acting ability that he also extricated himself from this situation.

Unbeknown to the king's party the alarm had been raised at Charmouth after the hostler at the inn had become suspicious. The party left the inn in the morning just before a troop of soldiers arrived. They had planned to take the road to London through Dorchester but in Bridport they had a late change of mind and decided to return to Trent, turning up a little used, narrow lane. Five minutes later the pursuing soldiers galloped past on the way to Dorchester! A small plaque now marks this spot where a spur of the moment decision saved the king's life.

They became hopelessly lost and paused outside a village inn while Colonel Wyndham enquired where they were. The village was

Above: The plaque on a cottage in the village of
Broadwindsor recording the visit of the fugitive king.

Broadwindsor and by luck the innkeeper was a loyal Royalist who agreed at once to let them stay the night using the room at the top of the inn. Naturally a cover story was concocted; the innkeeper did not realise how great a service he was doing the royalist cause!

The royal party had been through a lot, but their ordeal was not yet over. After settling down for what they hoped would be a peaceful night, some Commonwealth soldiers arrived at the inn and requisitioned all the remaining rooms. Charles and his companions were trapped on the top floor and in grave danger. Luck was on their side again. In the middle of the night a camp-follower went into labour and gave birth. The

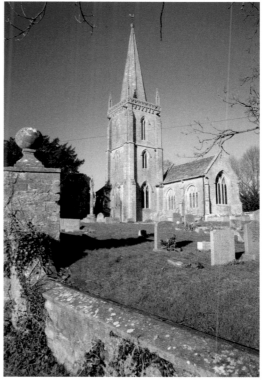

Above: The village church in Trent

commotion woke the whole village and there was much concern amongst the villagers that the soldiers would clear off and leave the child for the village to look after. After much heated discussion the soldiers were given the order to leave early in the morning. Seemingly the villagers got their way; the interests of the child and mother apparently counted for little. For Charles, of course, this was a very useful distraction and they were able to continue their way safely back to Trent.

The fugitives still had no idea why the ship had failed to materialise. It turned out that the captain, a man named Limbry, had told his wife that he had been given money to take a couple of gentlemen to France. She had been at Lyme fair and had heard the proclamation about the reward for the king's capture. Growing suspicious, she begged him not to go, fearing he might be caught and she left a widow. When the opportunity arrived, she locked him in his room and did not let him out till the morning!

After a few more days in Trent new plans were made that were to lead to the king's successful evacuation from Shoreham in Sussex. His days in Dorset made a lasting impression on the young monarch and after the Restoration he made many visits there, rewarding and remembering the people who had helped him. On one of these visits he passed through the village of Godmanstone where it is said he asked the smith for a glass of beer. The smith replied that he had no licence so Charles granted him one on the spot. The "Smith's Arms" is now one of several claiming to be the smallest pub in England.

Above and right: The Smith's Arms in Godmanstone, reputedly one of the smallest pubs in England. Originally a blacksmith's workshop, it was granted a licence by a thirsty King Charles II. Perhaps he didn't know that just up the road is the lovely village of Cerne Abbas with a long history of brewing beer and plenty of places to sample it!

The Monmouth Rebellion

After the execution of his father, Charles II had gone into exile on the continent, taking with him his mistress of the moment, Lucy Walter. In Rotterdam, in 1649, she bore him a son, James. Although illegitimate Charles recognised James as his son and, after the Restoration, took him with him to England. He soon began a career in the army which led to him becoming Colonel of the Life Guards and gaining recognition as one of the nation's finest soldiers. As a protestant many preferred him as heir to the throne to the king's brother James. However, in the absence of any legitimate son, Charles continued to recognise his brother as heir.

In 1683 James was forced to go to Holland in exile. When his father died in 1685, his uncle became James II of England. This was unpopular with protestants and mutterings of rebellion began to grow. In Holland James was encouraged to return to England to claim the throne, believing there would be a general uprising and that he would be supported by rebellions in Scotland and the north. Consequently, on the 11th June 1685, James, Duke of Monmouth stepped ashore at Lyme Regis at the head of about 400 men. In his honour the beach is now known as Monmouth Beach. He set off north, hoping to pick up reinforcements in strongly protestant Dorset and take Bristol, the second most important city in England. He eventually gathered an army of around 6000. As an expert commander James might have expected to achieve a great deal with a force of this size, but they were not experienced troops. Morale

Monmouth Beach at Lyme Regis, site of the Duke of Monmouth's landing in 1685, and also of executions in the aftermath of the rebellion.

Above left: Just over the border in Hampshire is a reminder of the terrible retribution presided over by Judge Jeffreys. Next to the entrance of Ellingham Church is the tomb of Dame Alice Lisle, a 71 year old lady who had sheltered two Monmouth supporters for a night. She was sentenced to death by Jeffreys and beheaded in Winchester.
Above right: The Monmouth Ash pub is in Verwood, near the place where Monmouth was captured.

soon plummeted and the ragged army was slaughtered at the Battle of Sedgemoor on 6 July, 1685. James had risked all in a daring night attack on the king's troops but the accidental discharge of a musket had alerted them.

James fled the battleground and attempted to make his way to Poole to get a ship to the continent. Once again a royal fugitive was hiding in the Dorset countryside. This time there were no swashbuckling adventures, James was found shivering in a ditch near the village of Horton. Legend has it that, although he had taken the precaution of wearing poor clothes, he had kept his badge of the Order of the Garter. This immediately revealed his identity and he was taken to London where he was beheaded at the Tower.

The aftermath of the rebellion has perhaps left a greater mark on history than the rebellion itself. This is certainly true for Dorset where the infamous Judge Jeffreys was sent to dispense justice to those who had supported the duke. Making his headquarters in Dorchester the judge began hearing what became known as the "Bloody Assizes". In an oak panelled room at the Antelope Hotel, Jeffreys dealt with about 300 rebels, sentencing most to death, although many had their sentence commuted to transportation as the government made money from the sale of slave labour. In the end 74 were executed, some were hanged and some suffered the terrible fate of being hung, drawn and quartered; their parts being dipped in pitch and sent to different parts of the county as a salutary display. In Weymouth, for example, 12 men were hung, drawn and quartered. For maximum effectiveness, the display of body parts was carefully organised. One head and six quarters were on show at the Grand Pier, one head and four quarters near the Esplanade and so on. The local authorities were forced to pay for the executions and associated constructions. It was not just those who had fought with Monmouth that were punished. In Weymouth a 14 year old boy who had read out the notice proclaiming the Duke of Monmouth as king was severely flogged.

In Lyme Regis 12 more rebels were hung on the beach where it had all started. Jeffreys attended these executions himself, staying in a house on Broad Street. His tormented ghost is reputed to haunt the spot.

The rebellion and its bloody aftermath had a profound effect on the county. Many suffered and communities were inevitably divided. To the relief of many, neither King James or his "Hanging Judge" lasted long, Jeffreys succumbing to a painful kidney disease and James being ousted by the successful coup led by William of Orange.

Left: The "Judge Jeffreys" restaurant in Dorchester where the "Bloody Assizes" were held.

The Dorset of Daniel Defoe

Daniel Defoe wrote what is generally regarded as the first English novel, *Robinson Crusoe*, published in 1719. What is less well-known is that in the 1720s he published a series of accounts of his extensive travels through England, Scotland and Wales. These provide a fascinating glimpse into a vanished age, just before the industrial revolution which dramatically changed the face of the British countryside and led to the growth of large urban areas. Defoe takes us on a tour through sleepy villages and market towns with downs populated by thousands of sheep, and along undeveloped coasts where the main activity was smuggling. This was an age before the seaside resort had become popular; hence there is no mention of Bournemouth on his travels through Dorset. Things had begun to change even during Defoe's lifetime with more of the population living in urban areas and London growing ever bigger and more important economically. A look at what Defoe has to say about Dorset is an enthralling step back in time. Below I have quoted what he had to say about some of Dorset's towns and countryside and compared them to how they appear today.

Any visitor to Christchurch cannot help but be struck by the town's affluence. You don't need to look in the estate agents' windows to realise that property prices here are well above the national average. The natural harbour teems with pleasure craft and in the summer the town is crammed with tourists. It boasts a wonderful priory and has

Looking towards Bournemouth from Hengistbury Head. Much of the coastline would have looked like this in Defoe's time.

Above: Poole Harbour - still full of craft.

a history going back beyond Saxon times when it was an important burgh or borough. It comes as something of a shock, then, when Defoe describes "Christ Church" as " a very inconsiderable poor place, scarce worth seeing and less worth mentioning in this account…". When talking about Lymington he had noted that "From hence there are but few towns on the sea coast west, nor are there any harbours, or sea ports of any note, except Pool." Clearly Bournemouth was not worth mentioning either!

In another of Dorset's ancient towns, Wimborne, Defoe again found "nothing remarkable, but the church". He noted that the church once had a spire, "finer and taller" than that of Salisbury Cathedral, which had blown down in 1622. Between Wimborne and Poole was a landscape that has now almost vanished. Defoe called it a "sandy, wild and barren country". Only small remnants of Dorset heathland now survive, much has been used for new housing and industrial estates.

Poole must have come as something of a shock for anyone travelling over the barren heathland; it was the most important port in this part of the country with ships from all over the world. Defoe notes particularly the valuable fishing in Newfoundland waters. Poole, apparently, was famous for its oysters which were barrelled up and sent as far away as the West Indies.

Wareham was summed up as a "neat town, and full of people". The Isle of Purbeck appears to have been quite well populated with Corfe Castle a thriving market town and the trade in Portland Stone is described as very profitable. What is noticeable from Defoe's descriptions is that the coastal areas were not well populated unless there was some sort of economic activity possible. Perhaps the most profitable activity all along the south coast was smuggling. Today's visitor travelling along the Dorset coast meets prosperous towns and villages, well kept and with many places to stay or eat and drink. It would have been very different in Defoe's time.

Dorchester was a town that impressed Defoe greatly. He found the town itself pleasant with broad streets, but it was the people who really left an impression on him. He notes, "there is good company and a good deal of it; and a man that coveted a retreat in this world might as agreeably spend his time, and as well in Dorchester, as in any town I know in England".

Weymouth was a "sweet, clean, agreeable town" with "a great many good substantial merchants in it". Presumably he was referring to their wealth and standing in the community rather than their size! Again it was trade which gave the town its prosperity, not tourism. Portland, of course, was famous in Defoe's time for the quarrying of building stone; considered the finest in England, it was extensively used in the rebuilding of London after the Great Fire. He describes the "island" as "seemingly miserable" but notes that the inhabitants were quite well off, being nearly all employed in the stone industry.

Left: Sherborne Abbey

Opposite right: A view across Cranborne Chase

Lime [Lyme Regis] was a prosperous port in Defoe's time, trading as far away as Newfoundland. It was [and is] famous as the landing place of James, Duke of Monmouth at the start of his ill-fated rebellion. Defoe tactfully mentions little of this, noting that it was still in living memory. He observes that the town has a number of prosperous merchants and that trade is considerable. He is clearly impressed by the Cobb which had existed in some form for many centuries and created Lyme's artificial harbour. At that time it consisted of two walls and Defoe states that it was big enough for warehouses and the Customs house to be built upon it.

Journeying inland Defoe describes Shireburn [Sherborne] as Dorset's most populous town and its church as a "reverend pile". Between Sherborne and Shaftesbury it is the vast flocks of sheep that make a deep impression on Defoe. Nowadays we are used to seeing large fields with perhaps a few flocks of sheep or herds of cattle, perfect country for the walker seeking to get away from it all. Not so in Defoe's time; there were literally hundreds of thousands of sheep on the downlands with shepherds who, according to Defoe were, "everywhere in the way, and who, with a very little pains, a traveller may always speak with." Defoe had been told at Dorchester that there were in the region of 600 000 sheep in the fields around the town and had seen no reason to doubt this. The countryside must indeed have presented a very different picture to what it does today and the foreign visitor can have been left in no doubt as to where England's wealth lay.

The 19th Century

The nineteenth century is remembered as the age of Victoria and the Industrial Revolution that brought vast wealth and power to the British Empire. In the popular imagination the cost of this development is often seen as the decline of an idyllic rural existence. In reality, although there was indeed a redistribution of the population away from the countryside and into huge urban areas, rural life was far from idyllic.

Dorset was not a county transformed by massive industrialisation, yet the changes here were just as dramatic. The writings of Thomas Hardy and the story of the Tolpuddle Martyrs have ensured that the deprivations of 19th century farm labourers are well-known.

Anyone who knows Dorset well is aware that scattered around the beautiful county are estates of landowners who once enjoyed vast wealth. In a government survey in the 1870s the largest landowner in Dorset was General Pitt-Rivers who had inherited the Rushmore Estate

and became a pioneer of modern archaeology with his excavations around Cranborne Chase. Other notable landowners included Walter Ralph Bankes of Corfe Castle and Kingston Lacy, the Earl of Shaftesbury at Wimborne St. Giles and the Sturts at Crichel. All in all, around three and a half thousand landowners owned over half a million acres between them. Most farmers were tenants who rented their farms from the wealthy few. The Enclosure Acts of the 18th and 19th centuries resulted in the major landowners fencing their land and denying the poor traditional rights of

Above: Cranborne Manor

Above: The Tolpuddle Martyrs' Museum

grazing. Some bad harvests in the 1820s resulted in the large numbers of farm labourers, those who earned their living from short-term jobs from the tenant farmers, becoming even more destitute.

In November 1830 in and around Cranborne, seat of the Marquis of Salisbury, a number of agricultural labourers rioted. There followed further outbreaks of violence around the county where farmers were threatened and threshing machines destroyed. These were part of what became known as the Captain Swing riots after a mysterious and probably mythical figure who wrote threatening letters to farmers and landowners. The riots had been provoked by the gradual introduction of horse-powered threshing machines which were perceived as a threat to the jobs of the labourers. Needless to say the authorities acted swiftly to subdue the riots; in Dorset 7 men were transported to Australia and 15 more jailed. Elsewhere in the country a number of men were hanged. The riots brought about little reform although the number of threshing machines did decline for a while until the advent of steam power and the unquenchable desire of the Victorians for "progress" resulted in farms becoming much more mechanised.

It is odd that the Captain Swing riots are not generally well-known and that a few years after them, in 1834, an impoverished farm labourer named James Loveless created a story that is known by millions and taught in every school. Loveless initiated the formation of a group or union of local labourers with the intention of increasing their bargaining power with local farmers. The group, in fact, broke no law but the authorities, frightened by the previous riots, trumped up charges of swearing an illegal oath and had the men transported to

Australia. Several years later, under pressure of public opinion, the men were reprieved. Only one, James Hammett, returned to live in Tolpuddle and he sadly died in the Dorchester workhouse in 1891. Today the Tolpudddle Martyrs are remembered as the founders of the Trade Union movement.

Although it is the sufferings of the rural poor in Dorset that attracted the attention of reformers, perhaps the county's greatest philanthropist was involved in the plight of those working in dreadful conditions in the factories of the industrial areas. Anthony Ashley Cooper, the 7th earl of Shaftesbury devoted his life to improving conditions for the thousands of young children working long hours in the difficult and dangerous environments of Victorian factories. The Ashley Coopers still own the magnificent mansion in Wimborne St. Giles, north of Wimborne.

The Quarrying Industry

Although Dorset was in the main an agricultural region it did have some large industries, the most important of which was quarrying. The Isle of Purbeck and the Isle of Portland both have outcrops of the world's best

building stone, the Portland Stone, strong, massive limestone deposited in the shallow tropical seas of the late Jurassic, over 100 million years ago. In both areas the thick horizontal layers of the rock are exposed along the coast. In Purbeck the stone was largely cut from galleries driven into the strata while on Portland huge, opencast works were sited on the high ground from where the stone was transported to the shore for shipping.

Exploring the coast from Durlston Head near Swanage westwards to St. Aldhelm's Head will teach you a lot about Dorset's quarrying industry. Here, in the magnificent cliffs, are many quarries that

Above: Remains of the Portland Stone quarry at Winspit.
Previous page top right: Almshouses built by the Ashley Coopers in
Wimborne St. Giles.
Previous page bottom left: The old village sign at Wimborne St. Giles

provided stone for some of London's most famous buildings. Small cranes known as "whims" were used to lower the stone onto waiting barges which then transported it to Swanage for loading onto bigger ships for export. It was dangerous work and could only be carried out in summer months when the weather allowed it. In 1893 it was reported that there were around 200 men working in 50 quarries in Purbeck, almost all with a different owner. Thus it was not such a labour intensive industry as might be imagined, given the lack of mechanisation. It was, however, a highly skilled occupation. The expertise of the quarrymen is legendary. They were a proud group with their own Royal Charter. Harry Ashley in his book *The Dorset Coast – History, Lore and Legend* recalls that the quarrymen used to go to work dressed like city gentlemen, changing into their work clothes at the quarry.

Earlier in the 19th century the quarry workings were put to good use by smugglers. The whims were ideal for unloading contraband and the caves and galleries ideal for hiding it. It is difficult to imagine that the quarrymen and even the quarry owners were not closely involved in this, no doubt welcoming the extra income and applauding the efficient use of the equipment they had invested in! Much of the wood used for supports in the caves and galleries came from the many shipwrecks around the Purbeck coast.

Portland was the more important source of stone in the 19th century. The census of 1851 showed that out of a male population of 2143 there were 480 quarrymen and 33 stonemasons. New technology seems to have played a greater part here with steam operated cranes and cutting saws. In 1865 the opening of a railway from Weymouth to Portland provided a means of transporting the stone inland.

1872 saw the completion of a breakwater of Portland Stone creating a sheltered anchorage for the Royal Navy. The work was mainly carried out by the inmates of Portland jail.

Some famous figures

A number of Dorset residents and natives have left a substantial legacy to the nation. Below are glimpses of just a few whose life stories provide fascinating reading.

Lewis Tregonwell was a successful army captain and commander of the Dorset Rangers. He was charged with catching smugglers and when, in 1810, his ailing wife saw the wild and remote coastline around the Bourne Stream she thought it an ideal place to recuperate. Tregonwell built her a villa there and followed it with several more. The town of Bournemouth began and has not looked back since. There are theories that Tregonwell was, in fact, in league with the smugglers and building a house in such an isolated area favoured by smugglers might tend to support the idea!

Anthony Ashley Cooper, the 7th earl of Shaftesbury, has already been mentioned and is rightly remembered as a leading philanthropist and reformer, doing more than anyone to relieve the plight of working children in Victorian mines and factories.

General Augustus Pitt-Rivers was a lucky man. After a distinguished military career he inherited his great uncle's vast estate at Rushmoor in 1880. Pitt-Rivers was an educated and curious man and became interested in his estate's many ancient remains. Fortunately he was also a patient and meticulous man and by his excavations of the burial barrows and Roman remains of Cranborne Chase he is credited with being the father of modern archaeology. Today the magnificent

Pitt-Rivers museum in Oxford displays many of his finds and details his work. Pitt-Rivers was also a philanthropist and was very keen that ordinary people should share his interest and the history that he uncovered. He also created the Larmer Tree gardens where people could enjoy picnics in beautiful surroundings and listen to music. This legacy lives on to this day and there is no better place to spend a sunny Sunday afternoon.

William Barnes [1801 –1886] was a distinguished clergyman and teacher. He is best remembered however as a leading poet, writing in Dorset dialect. It is Thomas Hardy, of course, who is Dorset's most famous literary figure. Born in 1840 he heard tales of smugglers from his parents and grandparents and witnessed for himself the hardship of life in rural Dorset and the changes brought about by increased mechanisation. His Wessex novels describe life in 19th century Dorset better than any history book.

Above: Part of the Larmer Tree Gardens laid out by General Pitt-Rivers. Visitors were encouraged to bring picnics and could even hire plates and cutlery.

In Conclusion

This book has only touched on some aspects of Dorset's colourful history but I hope it has shown that, when visiting the county's many beautiful locations, learning a little of this history can only enliven the occasion.

Consider the small, pretty Norman church in Studland on the south side of the entrance to Poole Harbour. This small community has witnessed Roman ships coming into and out of the harbour, has feared the appearance of Viking longships centuries later, has seen pirate ships anchor in Studland Bay and cooperated with the efforts of smugglers as they used the gently sloping beach to bring contraband ashore. There has been a place of worship here for centuries, possibly even before the Saxon church initiated by St. Aldhelm in the 7th century. This is a place with a long, dramatic and often tragic history, yet is now a place for relaxation and enjoyment. One man who chose to end his days in this tranquil setting in the 19th century was Serjeant William Lawrence, a veteran of the Napoleonic wars. His grave is near the entrance to the church and his headstone tells an almost unbelievable story. He fought in all of the major battles of the Peninsular campaign, being badly wounded at Badajoz after volunteering for the Forlorn Hope, the group first to attempt to storm the defences, and fought finally at Waterloo.

It is, perhaps, appropriate to finish our look at episodes in Dorset's history with the story of Sgt. Lawrence. After a long and often turbulent history Dorset has become a place where many people come to relax and savour the surroundings, either on holiday or sometimes for the rest of their lives.

Map of Dorset - showing location of places mentioned

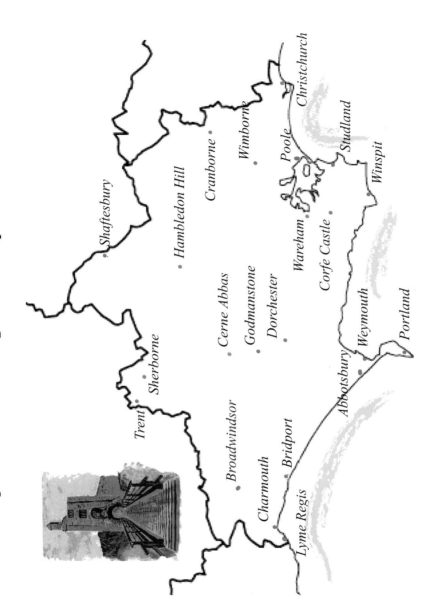

Further Reading and Bibliography

The Escape of Charles II after the Battle of Worcester - Richard Ollard, Constable and Robinson, 2002

King Stephen - Donald Matthew, Hambledon and London, 2002

The Dorset Village Book - Harry and Hugh Ashley, Countryside Books, 2000

The Victorians - Discover Dorset series - Jude James, The Dovecote Press, 1998

Lost Villages - Discover Dorset series - Linda Viner, The Dovecote Press, 2002

The Dorset Coast, History Lore and Legend - Harry Ashley, Countryside Books, 1992

Sherborne Old Castle - Peter White and Alan Cook, English Heritage, 1986

Dorset in the English Civil War - Robert Morris, Stuart Press, 1995

Ancient Dorset - Robert Westwood, Inspiring Places Publishing, 2006

Dark Age Dorset - Robert Westwood, Inspiring Places Publishing, 2007

A Tour Through the Whole Island of Great Britain - Daniel Defoe, edited by Pat Rogers, The Promotional Reprint Company Ltd., 1989